This Coloring Book belongs to

.....................Sophie...............

Coloring Book

Paul Gauguin

Prestel

Munich · London · New York

"How beautiful the South Seas are ..."

... thought Paul Gaugin, and decided to travel there. He wanted to live like a "primitive" and paint many beautiful pictures. And he did.

Gauguin's house on Tahiti. Photo: Charles Spitz

Paul Gauguin at the age of two

The artist was born in Paris in 1848. Even as a boy he dreamed of far-away lands and the simple life on the islands of the South Seas.

After earning a lot of money as a stock-broker and then losing everything, he left his wife and five children to paint.

He lived from hand to mouth. In the beginning only his artist friends like Vincent van Gogh thought his paintings were good. Most people at the time didn't know what to make of their flat areas and glowing colors. The figures were painted with such simple forms! But this was just what Paul Gauguin wanted: He did not want to copy reality, but "ponder and dream of" nature.

In this coloring book, you can see just how well he was able to do this.

Paul Gauguin with his children Clovis and Aline

Mette and Paul Gauguin

Good day, Monsieur Gauguin!

The country children in Brittany dance so cheerfully!

Many beautiful shrubs grown in the French town of Arles. Would you like to add some flowers?

Paul Gauguin longs to travel.

A mysterious life is waiting for him, but how far from home?

On the islands of the South Seas the fruits taste sweeter and the flowers bloom brighter!

Would you like to color the picture again, with your favorite colors?

When you go on a trip, you probably send postcards!
Would you like to send a greeting to your best friend?
You need only a pair of scissors, some colors,
and a stamp ...

This is what the postcards of Tahiti looked like during Paul Gauguin's lifetime.

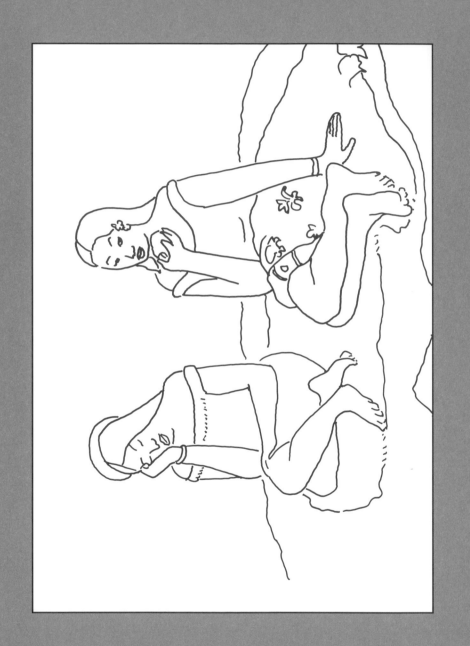

Here you can carefully bend the staples open and pull out the whole page.

Madam Giroux would have surely liked to get a letter!

Would you like to draw more of the village and the people who live there?

This soup doesn't look very good...

What do you like to eat most? Draw it in on the table!

Whom is the woman with the flowers thinking about?

Paul Gauguin liked white horses.
How would you color them?

Paint or draw more of the picture with beautiful, bright, South Seas colors!

Paul Gauguin feels at home when he's far away.

Goodbye, Monsieur Gauguin!

The original artworks by Paul Gauguin

Here you can see some of the artworks by
Paul Gauguin that were used as models
for this book.

Do you recognize them?

1 Tahitian Pastorale, 1895, Hermitage, St. Petersburg
2 Bonjour, Monsieur Gauguin, 1889, National Gallery, Prague
3 Breton Girls Dancing, 1888, National Gallery of Art, Washingotn
4 Woman with a Flower, 1891, Ny Carlsberg Glyptotek, Copenhagen
5 Miraculous Source, 1894, Hermitage, Saint Petersburg
6 The White Horse, 1898, Musée d'Orsay, Paris
7 Self Portrait Les Misérables,
   1888, Rijksmuseum Vincent van Gogh, Amsterdam
8 Night Café at Arles, 1888, Pushkin Museum
   of Fine Arts, Moscow

9 Landscape Farmhouse in Arles, 1888, National Museum, Stockholm
10 Old Women at Arles, 1888, The Art Institute,
   Collection of Mr. and Mrs. Lewis L. Coburn, Chicago
11 Arearea, aka Joyousness, 1891, Musée d'Orsay, Paris
12 The Meal, aka The Bananas, 1894, private collection
13 Midday Nap, 1894, private collection
14 When will You Marry? 1892, private collection
15 The Black Pigs, 1891, Museum of Art, Budapest
16 What news? 1892, Staatl. Kunstsammlungen,
   Gemäldegalerie Neue Meister, Dresden

© Prestel Verlag, Munich · London · New York, 2010. 2nd printing 2012

The series title, conception, and presentation of the series *Coloring Books* is protected by the laws of copyright and competition law.

Prestel, a member of Verlagsgruppe Random House GmbH

Prestel Verlag, Munich
www.prestel.de

Prestel Publishing Ltd.
4 Bloomsbury Place
London WC1A 2QA

Prestel Publishing
900 Broadway, Suite 603
New York, NY 10003
www.prestel.com

Prestel books are available worldwide. Please contact your nearest bookseller or one of the above addresses for information concerning your local distributor.

Concept, drawings, and texts: **Annette Roeder**

Picture editor: Andrea Jaroni
Translation and copyediting: Cynthia Hall
Design: Meike Sellier, Eching near Munich
Art direction: Cilly Klotz
Production: Nele Krüger
Lithography: ReproLine mediateam Munich
Printing and binding: Lanarepro GmbH, Lana

Verlagsgruppe Random House FSC-DEU-0100
The FSC-certified paper *Tauro* has been supplied by Papier Union GmbH, Germany.

ISBN 978-3-7913-7031-6

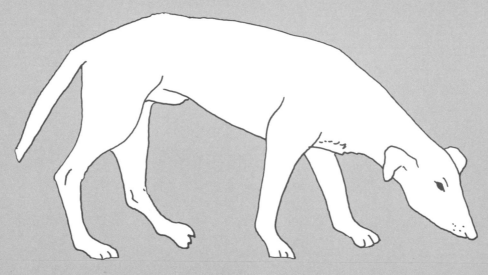